Financing educational systems: specific case studies—3

Included in the series: *

Country case studies

1. *Financing and educational policy in Sri Lanka (Ceylon)*
   J. Hallak

Specific case studies

1. *The financial aspects of first-level education in Iran*
   J. Hallak, M. Cheikhestani and H. Varlet
2. *Systèmes de prêts aux étudiants en Scandinavie*
   Maureen Woodhall
3. *Financing public first-level and second-level education in the U.S.A.*
   W.Z. Hirsch
4. *Organization and financing of self-help education in Kenya*
   J.E. Anderson

* Other titles to appear

Financing public first-level and second-level education in the U.S.A.

W.Z. Hirsch

Paris 1973
Unesco: International Institute for Educational Planning

Published in 1973 by the United Nations
Educational, Scientific and Cultural Organization
Place de Fontenoy, 75007 Paris
Cover designed by Dominic Toulec-Merten
Imprimerie Granchamps, Annemasse

ISBN 92 803 1053 4
LCNo. 72-94386

© Unesco 1973 IIEP 72/VIb.3/A
Printed in France

Aims and methodology of the IIEP research project on financing educational systems

This research project, launched by the International Institute for Educational Planning early in 1970, originated in an enquiry as to the real possibility of the developing countries financing their educational objectives in the course of the United Nations Second Development Decade, bearing in mind the high level of expenditure that has already been reached in most cases, the constant rise in unit costs, and the increasing competition within the state budgets themselves that education will probably encounter in the future from the financing of productive investments, debt servicing, and other predictable expenditures.

Viewed in this light, therefore, the research is not strictly limited to the study of financing techniques, but has wider aims:

1. To explore the real weight of probable financial constraints on the development of educational systems up to 1980.
2. To study the various financing methods likely to augment resources, and to define a strategy of educational financing more closely adapted to social and economic realities.
3. To analyse certain alternative solutions (new structures, new technologies, etc.) capable, by reducing costs or improving the efficiency of the teaching process, of leading to a better balance between educational targets and the resources available for them.

In addition to these extremely concrete objectives, concerned with the real problems facing educational planners in all countries, the collation of the essential data should provide the basis for the answers to more theoretical questions, affecting, for example, the type of correlation between educational expenditure and the level of development, between the level of expenditure and the method of financing, between the level of unit costs and the development of the educational system, etc.

With these aims in mind, two types of study are being undertaken:

1. *National case studies* for the *retrospective* (1961-70) and *prospective* (1980 or beyond) analysis of the expenditure, financing and costs of educational systems in the widest and most representative possible sample of countries—at least fifteen; these studies should, as already stated, reveal both the magnitude and the nature of the financial constraints to be expected in the general framework

Aims and methodology

of the development of the economy and of the finances of the state, and the level and various alternative forms for the possible development of educational systems. These studies will thus cover the whole field of educational financing, costs, and policies in each country concerned.
2. *Specific case studies* covering, first, the different possible methods of financing (centralised, decentralised, public, private, etc.) and, especially, original ways of raising supplementary resources, and, secondly, the study of new educational solutions calculated to reduce costs.

These studies are being carried out in Member States by the IIEP in close collaboration with national specialists, either from government departments or from universities; in many cases the research is a concerted effort by the IIEP and the country concerned, for the common benefit of both parties and of the international community as a whole.

This project will continue until 1973, and will culminate in a synthesis report summing up the findings relating to all the problems posed. A number of the studies have already been completed, however, and instead of presenting them in a single volume it has been decided to publish them as single monographs in a new collection, *Financing educational systems*, comprising two series, one of country case studies and one of specific case studies. The synthesis report will be published early in 1974.

The financial outlay for the implementation of this ambitious project could not be provided from Unesco's basic grant to the Institute. The IIEP is deeply grateful to the Member States and various organisations who, by their voluntary contributions, have enabled it to launch and pursue this research: in particular to SIDA (Swedish International Development Authority), NORAD (Norwegian Agency for International Development), DANIDA (Danish International Development Agency), CIDA (Canadian International Development Agency), the Republic of Ireland, and the Ford Foundation. The Institute is also deeply indebted to the Member States and national specialists in various parts of the world who have agreed to co-operate with the IIEP in carrying out these studies. The publication by the IIEP of certain studies by outside consultants does not necessarily imply, however, the Institute's agreement with all the opinions expressed in them.

Introduction

In most countries first- and second-level schools are financed, in the main, from the tax revenues of the State.[1] Centralised financing systems can be adapted to quite different forms of management; in some cases, such as France, the national education authorities control practically the entire use of national budget appropriations; in others, administration is decentralised to local authorities (towns, counties, districts, etc.) who nevertheless receive the bulk of their resources from the national budget, by transfer or otherwise (e.g. the United Kingdom, Russia, etc.).

The United States of America is an extreme case; both the financing and the administration of first- and second-level schools are highly decentralised among more than 25,000 school districts, and it is for this reason that the International Institute for Educational Planning has included the United States' experience in the list of specific studies of the financing of educational systems, the aims and methods of which have been set out in the foregoing general introduction.

In line with the purpose of our studies, Professor W.Z. Hirsch's work does not discuss questions of the management of educational establishments; it deals with all the problems raised by the decentralised financing of United States schools.

In the author's view, the decentralisation of the administration and financing of the United States education system has been inspired not by the specific needs of that system but by a political orientation expressing itself in mistrust of an all-powerful central government, and confidence in the capacity of the average citizen to administer those public services which directly affect him —first and foremost among them public education. The starting-point of the system of financing first- and second-level schools enshrined in American democracy from the outset seems to lie, therefore, in a decentralised conception of the State rather than in any specific consideration of the advantages or the possibilities of any particular method of financing. It is, however, by no means certain that in creating a highly decentralised administration, especially

---

1. Unitary, federal or federated state.

Introduction

in the matter of education, the Founding Fathers of the United States were not at the same time obeying the obvious practical considerations imposed by distance in that vast new country, as well as the imperatives of their own political philosophy.

In this connexion it may well be recalled that, forty years after the disappointing attempts of the French Revolution to create free, compulsory and state-financed popular education, the first foundations of the French primary school were laid by an Act of 1833 which, as in the United States, assigned to the most decentralised local authorities, the Communes (and, in part, to families) the responsibility for creating first-level schools and financing their development, subject only to a certain degree of State supervision. Unlike the American statesmen, the sponsors of the French Act of 1833 took their stand, not on any philosophy of decentralisation, but quite simply on the impossibility of financing first-level schools through the medium of State taxes—an impossibility which, in their view, had been demonstrated by the failure of the Revolution on this point.

Whatever its doctrinal origins, the financing systems of United States and French first-level schools did not radically differ during the first half of the nineteenth century; they were decentralised among small local authorities and the public funds were derived in both cases, as was normal at that time, from taxes assessed on landed property. Since then, however, the paths taken by the two countries have been very different.

From the end of the nineteenth century, in France, the costs of first-level schools and the responsibility for organising them were in all essentials taken over by the State, in accordance with the original objectives of the French Revolution, inspired by Jacobin ideology. Conversely, in the United States the financing system set up in the previous century had undergone very little change until after the Second World War.

W.Z. Hirsch throws little light on the history of the financing of first- and second-level schools in the United States or on the non-political motives which may originally have governed the choice of the American authorities; indeed, that was not his purpose. He plunges into the midst of the problems raised by the survival of such a system two hundred years after it was created, in a new world where the relative importance of the political, social, economic and even geographic factors which justified earlier choices has radically changed.

In this connexion W.Z. Hirsch's study may not appear particularly laudatory of the system which it describes; its purpose seems rather to be to analyse the possible ways and means of correcting the disadvantages of a decentralised financing system than to try to justify it.

It is, indeed, important that the reader should place himself clearly in the historical context we have recalled. Originally justified by a political policy of decentralisation, and, to all appearances, by other more concrete factors, the United States decentralised administrative system has to adjust itself to the realities of this second half of the twentieth century. From this point of view, without challenging principles to which the American people are quite obviously still attached, W.Z. Hirsch points out the difficulties encountered in a modern democracy by an educational system with highly decentralised sources of finance, and analyses the steps taken to try to remedy them. That is the value of this study now published by the IIEP.

The author's analysis covers two main fields: first, the nature of the various resources which the school districts are in a position to mobilise; second, the justification for, and instruments of, the increasing intervention of the States in the financing of first- and second-level schools.

On the first point the author shows how some of the difficulties at present felt in financing school districts from a property tax have led to a search for other sources of tax revenue, the nature and volume of which vary according to the State. Similarly, financial aid from the States to the school districts takes concrete form in the payment of many different categories of grants, whose number, purposes and rates depend on criteria specific to the different States.

Under the United States Constitution, moreover, education is within the exclusive competence of the States; in the light of considerations of national importance, however, a number of Acts passed by the United States Congress have authorised the intervention of the Federal Government in the financing of the education system, including certain aspects of general education. This source of finance, however, though growing, still remains relatively marginal.

In the last analysis, the financing of United States first- and second-level schools still remains largely decentralised, but does not constitute a homogeneous or uniform system. On the contrary, it makes use of a wide range of solutions. It is the great merit of Professor W.Z. Hirsch that he has so clearly presented a state of affairs whose complexity and diversity should provide food for thought by specialists in the financing of education systems.

RAYMOND POIGNANT
Director, IIEP

Contents

I. Introduction and summary	13
II. The present and past of the American public first- and second-level educational system	15
III. Local financial support	22
The nature of property taxes	22
School property taxes	27
Non-property taxes raised by local school districts	29
IV. Intergovernmental fiscal relations	30
Intergovernmental fiscal instruments	30
V. State support for schools	33
Flat grants	33
Flat grants in conjunction with categorical aid	33
Matching grants	34
Equalization grants	34
Details on grant programmes in two states	36
VI. Federal support for schools	43
Vocational Education Act	44
Science Education Acts	44
Federal Impact School Aid Acts	45
Federal aid to equalize educational opportunity	45
VII. Opportunities and prospects	48

I. Introduction and summary

Public education in the United States is a very large enterprise of about forty-five million pupils, about two million teachers, and about $30 thousand million expenditure in 1970. Not only is it a large industry, but public education has been growing very rapidly in the postwar period; there are, however, signs that the rate of growth is slowing down. By tradition, public education in the United States has been highly decentralized. Today's federated political and fiscal structure, which assigns major first-level and second-level educational decisions and financing responsibilities to local school districts, was generally formulated almost two centuries ago. In those days of physical isolation, individualism and self-determination, each community raised funds to finance its services, and virtually all cost burdens and benefits stayed within its boundaries. Today, however, the United States enjoys great specialization of economic activity — and therefore economic interdependence — rapid mobility, and advanced industrialization and urbanization. Under such conditions, widespread intercommunity spillovers are prevalent. Spillovers occur if any portion of the benefits or costs of a government service that is provided in one jurisdiction is realized by residents of another. They are external effects, imposed or freely given and unearned or unavoided by receivers.

Education is a merit good, which should be made available to everyone regardless of his income and therefore his ability to afford it. Thus its financing is best carried out by governments that can redistribute income in a major way, i.e., the federal and (to a lesser extent) the state governments. In spite of education's merit good characteristics, in spite of large differences in the fiscal capacity of school districts and states, and also large-scale spillovers, education in the United States has been financed mainly by local government. Here rests one of the major problems of the public education enterprise. Almost exclusive reliance on property taxes by local school districts is the source of much of the difficulty facing public education in the United States today. The property tax, because it is property- and not people-oriented, is not the best means of financing the education of the young. Also increases in the property tax rate, as well as school bond issues, need to be approved by popular elections. Furthermore, the property tax is usually substantially less flexible than expenditure for public education.

These characteristics of the property tax, together with a diminishing confidence on the part of the American electorate in the ability of the educational enterprises to provide high quality education efficiently, led in the late 1960s to what has often been described as a taxpayers' revolt.

Under those conditions the solution to fiscal difficulties appears strikingly clear—shifting more of the financing of education on to state and federal governments. The federal government, however, after almost doubling its aid to first- and second-level education from 1964/65 to 1965/66, has been reluctant to make further major increases during the following five years. And as long as the United States is engaged in the Vietnam war and suffers tremendous inflationary pressures, it appears that domestic programmes, including education, will be hard pressed to find additional federal financing. Yet, state governments in the United States have also increased their share of funds for education, from 37.3 per cent in 1963/64 to 40.7 per cent in 1968/69. However, in a number of states, including the state of California, state participation in the financing of public first- and second-level education has been declining in recent years.

We would be oversimplifying matters if we assumed that state and federal financing of education would solve all the problems of education, or that in the absence of solutions to key educational problems such funding is likely to result. Specifically, in the postwar period the educational system in the United States suffered from exceedingly rapid growth with its various by-products—archaic structures, hardening of the arteries, insufficient responsiveness to local needs and attitudes, procedures that alienate pupils and parents, inefficiency, etc. These are some of the difficult problems for which American education will have to seek solutions if it hopes to be financed properly and to make effective use of such funds.

II. The present and past of the American public first- and second-level educational system

The United States educational system is not only large but also highly decentralized. In 1970, public schools were educating about forty-five million first- and second-level school pupils with the aid of about two million teachers and a budget of about $30 thousand million a year.[1] An additional seven million pupils are enrolled in private schools. About 25 per cent of the population is attending school.

The public educational system in the United States has also incurred rapid growth. Thus during the eleven-year period, 1955/56 to 1966/67, public school enrolment increased from thirty-one million to forty-four million pupils (see Table 1). Enrolment growth took place not only because of growth in the school-age population but also because of a major increase in the percentage of five-, sixteen-, and seventeen-year-olds enrolled in schools. For example, in 1947, just over half of the five-year-olds were enrolled in school — including kindergarten — while twenty years later it had grown to just about 75 per cent. During the same period similar figures for sixteen- and seventeen-year-olds changed from just below 70 to just below 90 per cent. However, as can be seen in Table 1 the annual percentage increase in enrolment has been declining in recent years.

The number of teachers employed by public education has more than doubled during the last thirty years. Thus, for example, in 1939/40 less than 900,000 teachers were employed, whereas by 1967/68 this number had increased to almost 1,900,000 (see Table 2), with another 220,000 teachers in private schools.

The United States educational system is highly decentralized as a result of the early influence of Thomas Jefferson, who insisted that government should be close to the people. Philosophically, Jefferson warned, 'When all government... shall be drawn to Washington as the center of all power, it... will become as venal and oppressive as the government from which we separated.'[1] Materialistically, he contended, 'If ever this vast country is brought under a

---

1. Advisory Commission on Intergovernmental Relations, *State aid to local government*, Washington D.C., 1969 (pp. 31-34).
2. H.A. Washington, ed., *The writings of Thomas Jefferson*, Washington D.C., U.S. Congress, 1853-54. (Vol. VII, p. 126).

TABLE 1. Enrolment in public first- and second-level schools 1955/56 to 1966/67 with projections for 1970 and 1975 (in thousands)

School year	Number	Percentage increase over previous year	School year	Number	Percentage increase over previous year
1955/56	31 162		1962/63	39 746	3.9
1956/57	32 334	3.8	1963/64 [1]	41 025	3.2
1957/58	33 529	3.7	1964/65 [1]	42 280	3.1
1958/59	34 839	3.9	1965/66 [1]	42 023	1.8
1959/60	36 087	3.6	1966/67 [1]	43 955	2.2
1960/61	37 260	3.2	1970 [1]	45 300	—
1961/62	38 253	2.7	1975 [1]	44 700	—

1. Estimated
SOURCE Adapted from Office of Education, *Digest of educational statistics*, 1967 and *Education in the seventies*, Washington D.C., U.S. Department of Health, Education and Welfare, 1967

TABLE 2. Number of teachers in public first- and second-level schools, selected years 1939/40 to 1968 (in thousands)

Year	Kindergarten — grade 8	Grades 9-12	Total
1939/40	575	300	875
1949/50	590	325	915
1959/60	834	521	1 355
1966/67	1 017	787	1 804
1967/68	1 039	820	1 859

SOURCE Adapted from *Digest of educational statistics*, op. cit.

single government, it will be one of the most extensive corruption — indifferent and incapable of a wholesome care.'[1] In accordance with this philosophy, the United States relies heavily on highly decentralized school districts, amounting to more than 100,000 at the beginning of World War II. In spite of major efforts to consolidate small school districts into larger ones, there were still about 23,000 school districts in the United States in 1967.[2]

Although in the last twenty-five years the number of school districts has thus been greatly reduced, some states, including the relatively sparsely-populated state of South Dakota, have more than 1,000 independent school districts. Nevertheless, of the 23,000 independent school districts fewer than 9,000 account

1. Ibid., Vol. VII, p. 256.
3. *U.S. Census of government, 1967.*

for 58 per cent of the total pupils enrolled in public first- and second-level schools. Local school districts are agents of the state. Thus the state government imposes a variety of rules and obligations; it also delegates specified, limited taxing powers to the districts.

Such a large enterprise as education obviously involves very large funds. Thus in 1966/67 direct outlays for first- and second-level education amounted to $32 thousand million, of which local governments raised more than $15 thousand million, state governments somewhat less than $11 thousand million, and the federal government about $2 thousand million; the rest came from earnings of schools, including tuition (see Table 3). To this figure of $32 thousand million $8 to $12 thousand million might be added as indirect costs incurred by students who, while attending school, are foregoing earnings.[1]

If one takes this broad view of the cost of formal first- and second-level education, one finds that it accounted for in excess of 5 per cent of gross national product (GNP) in the late 1960s.[2] The claim of public first- and second-level education on GNP has doubled in the last two decades.

State aid for local schools, including federal aid channelled through the states, has been increasing, and reached almost $12 thousand million in 1967. As a percentage of state and local general expenditures for all purposes, state education aid now exceeds 12 per cent; as a percentage of local school expenditures

TABLE 3. Costs of formal education, 1966/67 ($ thousand million)

Item	Total	First- and second-level education	Third-level education
Direct outlays	48.8	32.0	16.8
Student tuition and fees	3.6	0.9	2.7
State governments	14.7	10.7	4.0
Local governments	15.7	15.3	0.4
Federal government	6.1	2.3	3.8
Endowment, charity, and earnings of institutions	8.7	2.8	5.9
Indirect costs: foregone earnings of students	20-30	8-12	12-18

SOURCE *The annual report of the council of economic advisers*, op. cit.

1. Council of Economic Advisers, *The annual report of the council of economic advisers, 1967*, Washington D.C., Government Printing Office, 1967 (p. 144).
2. In accounting for school finances, one can follow either of two sets of books. One set is maintained by the school systems and summarized by the U.S. Office of Education; it contains the amounts as seen by public school officials. The other set is maintained by the collecting and disbursing officials of the units of government and summarized in reports of the U.S. Census of Governments. The dollar amounts in each set, for apparently similar items, are not always easily reconciled. School officials tend to work with figures based on school years, whereas state governors and legislators and the U.S. Bureau of the Census work with figures based on fiscal years.

it exceeds 40 per cent (see Table 4). While the trend of the local share of public spending has been downward and amounts now to about 52 per cent, the share of state and particularly of federal contributions has been increasing (see Table 5). As can be seen in Table 6, there are great differences in the particular manner each state funds its public schools.

TABLE 4. General expenditure of state and local governments and local school expenditures 1957-67 ($ million)

Year	State and local general expenditures	Local school[1] expenditures	School as percentage of general expenditures	State education aid	State education aid as percentage	
					General expenditures	Local school expenditures
1957	40 375	11 547	28.9	4 212	10.4	36.1
1958	44 851	13 032	29.1	4 598	10.3	35.3
1959	48 887	14 034	28.7	4 957	10.1	35.3
1960	51 876	15 166	29.2	5 461	10.5	36.0
1961	56 201	16 608	29.6	5 963	10.6	35.9
1962	60 206	17 739	29.5	6 474	10.8	36.5
1963	64 816	18 802	29.0	6 993	10.8	37.2
1964	69 302	20 399	29.4	7 664	11.1	37.6
1965	75 446	21 966	29.5	8 351	11.2	38.0
1966	82 843	25 091	30.3	10 177	12.3	40.6
1967	93 770	28 066	29.9	11 845	12.6	42.2

1. Census data exclude debt service and certain other charges which are included in the Office of Education tabulation.
SOURCE U.S. Bureau of Census, *Governmental Finances*.

TABLE 5. Governmental sources of financing for public first- and second-level schools, 1963/64 to 1968/69 ($ thousand million)

Year	Federal		State		Local		Total
	Amount	Percentage	Amount	Percentage	Amount	Percentage	
1963/64	1.4	4.6	8.1	37.3	12.6	58.1	22.1
1964/65	1.1	4.3	8.7	37.0	13.8	58.7	23.5
1965/66	2.1	8.0	9.7	36.9	14.5	55.1	26.3
1966/67	2.3	8.1	10.8	37.8	15.4	54.1	28.5
1967/68	2.4	8.1	11.3	37.8	16.2	54.1	29.9
1968/69	2.5	7.3	13.7	40.7	17.5	52.0	33.7

SOURCE *Digest of educational statistics*, op. cit.
National Educational Association, *Estimates of school statistics*, 1968/69 (Research report 1963-R16, copyright 1968 by the National Education Association, all rights reserved)

TABLE 6. Estimated revenue receipts for first- and second-level schools, 1968/69

State and region	Revenue receipts by source (in thousands)				Percentage of revenue receipts by source [1]					
					Total			Excluding Federal		
	Federal [2]	State	Local and other [3]	Total	Federal [2]	State	Local		State	Local
New England	111 391	498 576	1 272 825	1 882 792	5.9	26.5	67.6		28.1	71.9
Connecticut	25 000	178 000	365 000	568 000	4.4	31.3	64.3		32.8	67.2
Maine	9 944	47 930	80 057	137 931	7.2	34.7	58.0		37.5	62.5
Massachusetts	60 000	195 000	616 000	871 000	6.9	22.4	70.7		24.0	76.0
New Hampshire	4 770	8 780 [4]	83 342	96 892	4.9	9.1 [4]	86.0		9.8	90.2
Rhode Island	8 158	43 866	72 647	124 671	6.5	35.2	58.3		37.6	62.4
Vermont	3 519	25 000	55 779	84 298	4.2	29.7	66.2		30.9	69.1
Mideast	462 422	3 577 651	4 391 612	8 431 685	5.5	42.4	52.1		44.9	55.1
Delaware	8 000	78 500	21 500	108 000	7.4	72.7	19.9		78.2	21.8
Maryland	52 540	291 295	437 724	781 559	6.7	37.3	56.0		39.9	60.1
New Jersey	60 000	359 000	886 000	1 305 000	4.6	27.5	67.9		28.8	71.2
New York	176 000	1 993 000	1 997 000	4 166 000	4.2	47.8	47.9		49.9	50.1
Pennsylvania	103 563	855 856	933 264	1 892 683	5.5	45.2	49.3		47.8	52.2
Dist. of Columbia *	62 319 [5]		116 124	178 443	34.9 [5]	...	65.1			100.0
Southeast	718 690	3 272 790	1 855 114	5 846 594	12.3	56.0	31.7		63.4	36.6
Alabama	58 000	219 000 [6]	88 000	365 000	15.9	60.0 [6]	24.1		71.3	28.7
Arkansas	38 000	105 210	82 000	225 210	16.9	46.7	36.4		56.1	43.9
Florida [7]	101 279	563 275	332 436	996 990	10.2	56.5	33.3		62.9	37.1
Georgia	64 931	372 307 [8]	151 427	588 665	11.0	63.2 [8]	25.7		71.1	28.9
Kentucky	65 000	211 000	135 000	411 000	15.8	51.3	32.8		61.0	39.0
Louisiana	61 000	373 275	160 000	594 275	10.3	62.8	26.9		70.0	30.0

continued overleaf

* Estimated by NEA Research Division.
1. Percentage may not add up to 100 due to rounding.
2. Includes federal grant programmes to state and local school systems, including funds under the Elementary and Secondary Education Act, Economic Opportunity Act, Aid to Federally Impacted Areas, National Defense Education Act, Manpower Development and Training, Vocational Education, etc. Funds received from the School Lunch and Milk Programme are included, but reporting on the money value of commodities received is incomplete. ESEA revenues have generally been estimated on an anticipated cash expenditure basis at a level similar to outlays in the previous year.
3. Includes revenue receipts from local and intermediate sources, gifts, and tuition fees from patrons.
4. Excludes state's share of teacher retirement and social security.
5. Includes federal appropriations for capital outlays, civil defense, Capital Page School, and other federally funded programmes listed in footnote 2.
6. Includes social security and teacher retirement for all educational agencies and institutions.
7. Excludes revenues for public junior colleges which are operated by a junior college district board of trustees.
8. Includes state payments of $20,681,820 for teacher retirement.

TABLE 6. Continued.

State and region	Revenue receipts by source (in thousands)				Percentage of revenue receipts by source [1]				Excluding Federal	
	Federal [2]	State	Local and other [3]	Total	Federal [2]	Total State	Local	State	Local
Southeast continued										
Mississippi	58 980	156 923	79 651	295 554	20.0	53.1	26.9	66.2	33.8
North Carolina	83 000	434 000	128 000	645 000	12.9	67.3	19.8	77.2	22.8
South Carolina	41 000	215 000	82 000	338 000	12.1	63.6	24.3	72.4	27.6
Tennessee	55 000	224 800	182 000	461 800	11.9	48.7	39.4	55.3	44.7
Virginia	65 000	285 000	350 000	700 000	9.3	40.7	50.0	44.9	55.1
West Virginia	27 500	113 000	84 600	225 100	12.2	50.2	37.6	57.1	42.9
Great Lakes									
Illinois	324 443	2 247 145	4 204 495	6 776 083	4.8	33.2	62.0	34.8	65.2
Indiana	95 406	486 329	1 241 093	1 822 828	5.2	26.7	68.1	28.1	71.9
Michigan	44 000	309 000	555 000	908 000	4.8	34.0	61.1	35.8	64.2
Ohio	67 000	752 464	877 913	1 697 377	3.9	44.3	51.7	46.1	53.9
Wisconsin	84 400	510 000	1 025 000	1 619 400	5.2	31.5	63.3	33.2	66.8
	33 637	189 352	505 489	728 478	4.6	26.0	69.4	27.2	72.8
Plains									
Iowa [4]	174 503	860 501	1 559 616	2 594 620	6.7	33.2	60.1	35.6	64.4
Kansas	20 300	156 000	302 700	479 000	4.2	32.6	63.2	34.0	65.6
Minnesota	31 928	118 758	256 295	406 981	7.8	29.2	63.0	31.7	68.3
Missouri	45 000	294 000	340 000	679 000	6.6	43.3	50.1	46.4	53.6
Nebraska	40 868	222 193	385 121	648 182	6.3	34.3	59.4	36.6	63.4
North Dakota	14 257	33 000	140 000	187 257	7.6	17.6	74.8	19.1	80.9
South Dakota	7 750	25 550	64 500	97 800	7.9	26.1	66.0	28.6	71.4
	14 400	11 000	71 000	96 400	14.9	11.4	73.7	13.4	86.6
Southwest									
Arizona	268 476	1 095 797	964 009	2 328 282	11.5	47.1	41.4	53.2	46.8
New Mexico	22 089	151 705	101 113	274 907	8.0	55.2	36.8	60.1	39.9
Oklahoma	29 089	119 212 [5]	44 546	192 847	15.1	61.8 [5]	23.1	72.6	27.4
Texas [6]	42 000	115 000	195 000	352 000	11.9	32.7	55.4	37.1	62.9
	175 298	709 880	623 350	1 508 528	11.6	47.1	41.3	53.3	46.7

Rocky Mountains	68 664	275 648	496 375	840 687	8.2	32.8	59.0	35.8	64.2
Colorado	26 000	88 000	252 000	366 000	7.1	24.0	68.9	25.9	74.1
Idaho*	9 575	42 000	51 000	102 575	9.3	40.9	49.7	45.2	54.8
Montana*	9 000	35 000	83 000	127 000	7.1	27.6	65.4	29.7	70.3
Utah	11 089	94 648	76 375	182 112	6.1	52.0	41.9	55.6	44.4
Wyoming	13 000	16 000	34 000	63 000	20.6	25.4	54.0	32.0	67.8
Far West	290 492	1 736 669	2 770 939	4 798 100	6.1	36.2	57.8	38.5	61.5
California	215 000	1 260 000	2 200 000	3 675 000	5.9	34.3	59.9	36.4	63.6
Nevada	6 500	35 300	49 100	90 900	7.2	38.8	54.0	41.7	58.3
Oregon	28 992	79 369	326 839	432 200	6.7	17.7	75.6	18.9	81.1
Washington	40 000	365 000	195 000	600 000	6.7	60.8	32.5	65.2	34.8
Alaska	18 830	32 780	21 700	73 310	25.7	44.7	29.6	59.3	40.7
Hawaii	15 300	130 000	8 000	153 300	10.0	84.8	5.2	94.2	5.8
50 States and D.C.	2 453 211	13 727 557	17 544 685	33 725 453	7.3	40.7	52.0	43.9	56.1

1. See footnote 1, page 19.
2. See footnote 2, page 19.
3. See footnote 3, page 19.
4. Includes state appropriations for area vocational schools and junior colleges.
5. Includes revenues for operation of the Public School Finance Division which is not part of the state department of education.
6. Excludes revenues for kindergarten.
* Estimated by NEA Research Division.

SOURCE: National Education Association, *Estimates of school statistics, 1968/69,* Research Report, 1968, R. 16

III. Local financial support

Since the early 1940s state and local taxes in the United States have steadily declined as percentages of total general revenue, while the percentages of miscellaneous general revenue and federal aid have increased. In the late 1960s less than 70 per cent of the general revenue of state and local governments came from their own tax collections; the rest was distributed about equally between miscellaneous general revenue and federal aid (see Table 7). Among the various state and local government taxes in the late 1960s, the property tax (although its percentage has been declining) is still the single most important tax, accounting for almost one-half of all tax receipts. It is followed by sales and gross receipts taxes, which account for a little less than 30 per cent, and income tax, which yields about 15 per cent.

In the United States the power to levy taxes is not inherent in the school district or in any local governmental unit. This power is granted expressly by the state legislature to the school districts which it has created. School districts may not tap new tax sources without the express authorization of the legislature.

The largest single source of revenue collected locally by school districts is the property tax. In most school districts, more than four-fifths of revenues collected locally come from this source; indeed, for the large majority of school districts this is the only local tax source available. In a minority of states legislatures have empowered local taxing authorities to levy certain non-property taxes such as a local income tax, a local sales tax, or a tax on the rental of hotel rooms or on restaurant meals. The levying of these taxes is a matter of local option inaugurated after the endorsing vote of the majority of the electors. In only one state, Pennsylvania, are such non-property taxes widely used by school districts in the support of public education. Other — although minor — revenue sources are tuition income from non-resident students who attend district schools, and charges for lunch programmes, auditorium use, etc.

The nature of property taxes

A property tax is a governmental levy on certain physical or tangible assets that are claims to future services, as opposed to intangible or financial assets

TABLE 7. State and local sources of general revenue, selected years, 1942-67 ($ millions)

	1942		1948		1957		1960		1963		1965		1967	
	Amount	%	Amount	%	Amount	%	Amount	%	Amount	%	Amount	%	Amount	%
Federal aid	858	8.2	1 861	10.8	3 843	10.0	6 974	13.8	8 663	13.9	11 029	14.8	15 505	16.9
Taxes	8 528	81.9	13 342	77.3	28 817	75.5	36 117	71.5	44 014	70.7	51 578	69.4	61 241	66.8
Individual income	276	2.6	543	3.1	1 753	4.6	2 463	4.9	3 267	5.2	4 090	5.5	5 835	6.4
Corporation income	272	2.6	592	3.4	984	2.6	1 180	2.3	1 505	2.4	1 929	2.6	2 227	2.4
Sales and gross receipts	2 351	22.6	4 442	25.8	9 467	24.8	11 849	23.5	14 446	23.2	17 118	23.0	20 554	22.4
Property	4 537	43.6	6 126	35.5	12 864	33.7	16 407	32.5	19 833	31.8	22 918	30.8	26 280	28.6
Other taxes	1 092	10.5	1 638	9.5	3 733	9.7	4 218	8.3	4 963	8.0	5 523	7.4	6 345	6.9
Miscellaneous general revenue	1 031	9.9	2 047	11.9	5 503	14.4	7 414	14.7	9 593	15.4	11 735	15.8	14 881	16.2
Total general revenue:														
Amount in current prices	10,418	100.0	17 250	100.0	38 163	100.0	50 504	100.0	62 269	100.0	74 341	100.0	91 627	100.0
Percentage of GNP	6.5%		6.6%		8.6%		10.0%		11.1%		11.0%		11.6%	
Percentage of national income	7.6%		7.7%		10.4%		12.2%		12.9%		13.4%		14.1%	
Per capita in current prices	$77.25		$117.64		$224.09		$280.59		$330.07		$383.61		$463.08	
Per capita in constant prices [1]	$143.06		$133.83		$226.35		$278.64		$329.08		$374.25		$436.46	

1. Deflated by Bureau of Labour Statistics Wholesale price index (1957-59 = 100)

SOURCES Laszlo Ecker-Racz, 'A foreign scholar ponders at the 1957 census of governments', in *National tax journal*, Vol. 12, June 1959. (p. 107)
  Economic report of the President, Washington D.C., 1966. (pp. 207, 215, 221)
  U.S. Bureau of Census, *Statistical abstract*: 1963, (p. 422); 1966, (p. 5, 423); 1968, (p. 341); Washington D.C., various years.
  Advisory Commission on Intergovernmental Relations, *State and local finances: significant features 1966-1969*, Washington D.C., 1968. (p. 17, 19)
  U.S. Department of Commerce, *Survey of current business*, Vol. 49, February 1969, (p. S-1ff)

that are claims to future receipts of money. The tangible assets most heavily taxed are real property and, to a lesser extent, personal property. Real property is primarily land, structures, fences, irrigation systems, and other long-lived assets attached permanently (or nearly so) to a particular site. Real property taxes are impersonal levies, whereas personal property taxes are personal levies.

Since the possession of financial assets, such as common stocks, represents a claim to money returns on real corporate assets but does not embody legal title to the real assets themselves, it is exempted from property taxes. Furthermore, it is hard to discover and to add to the tax base. Thus, if property taxes were levied on the real corporate assets, the corporation itself would be liable, but if personal property taxes were levied on the owner of common shares, additional liabilities would be created against the incomes flowing from the same real corporate assets.

Although property taxes have frequently been criticized and their general demise has often been predicted, they have been a major source of state and local revenue for a long time. Property tax revenues rose from $4.5 thousand million in 1942 to about $31.5 thousand million in 1969. Even though absolute property tax collections increased substantially during this period, their percentage of state and local general revenue declined — from 44 per cent of all revenue in 1942 to 29 per cent in 1967 (see Table 7). Nevertheless the property tax provides about two-thirds of the revenue from all local sources and seven-eighths of local tax revenues.

The predominance of real property taxes as a source of local governmental revenue is directly related to one of the tax's key features, tax base immobility. Fear of tax avoidance via migration or commuting to neighbouring communities has significantly deterred local governments from diversifying their tax bases.

A number of states give *partial* exemptions from the local general property tax to specific owners (homestead loans, veterans' exemptions, and others). Although most states have a relatively insignificant set of partial exemptions, in aggregate they amount to one-sixth to one-quarter of gross assessed evaluations. Much real property is completely exempted; e.g., property belonging to religious and charitable organizations or owned by other governments. Property owned by the federal government is completely outside the state and local property tax base. The federal government, however, in some cases makes adjustment payments to local governments in lieu of taxes.

Some local governmental services may be of benefit to some members of the community but detrimental to property owners. For example, highway improvements that benefit residents by allowing better and more rapid movements about the city can lead to a decline in the value of certain lands and buildings close to these highways. But, in general, local services tend to be site-oriented and much of the benefit received by citizens can be taxed by levying liabilities on real property.

The link between real property tax burdens and the benefits received from local governmental services holds for commercial, philanthropic, religious, and agricultural property owners as well as residential property owners. Real property taxes on similar assets do not ordinarily discriminate between differences in the owners' ability to pay. And, in general, real property holdings are a poor proxy for ability to pay since debt liabilities are ignored.

James Buchanan argues that the property tax, as it is administered, has a great advantage in that it can be broken down into separate rates (*mill* rates), which can be applied to each public agency or function for which revenues from the tax are earmarked. Rarely do taxpayers get this sort of information or the opportunity to weigh the relative costs of separate public functions one against the other.[1]

Another feature contributing to the popularity of property taxation in the past has been revenue stability, largely the product of persistent urban growth and of assessment practices. Infrequent and delayed property reassessment prevents the tax base from shrinking when local economic activity declines and from rising rapidly when such activity increases. Thus large revenue fluctuations are uncommon. But the long-run effect of steadily increasing property tax rates may be more unsettling. It is generally held that in the long run property taxation discourages renewal of urban property and encourages location of improvement investments outside urban tax jurisdictions (especially local school jurisdictions). At the same time, local expenditures on non-property-related services may have increased.

Empirical studies have assumed that property taxes on residential property are almost entirely borne by the present owners. But they may have purchased the taxed assets at tax-discounted prices, and thus past owners may have borne much of the burden of tax changes. For non-residential property, empirical studies have almost always assumed that the entire amount of the tax burden is passed on even though this practice is not supported by the results of theoretical analysis. The owners of non-residential property at the time of tax increases on their assets will suffer decreases in their wealth positions, just as owners of residential property do under the same circumstances. But we have some reason to believe that non-residential asset owners will be more able to pass on tax burdens than residential owners. Much of the supposed regressiveness in property taxes appears to be due to the assumption that rental property and business property taxes are almost completely passed on, predominantly to the tenant or customer. It has also been reasoned that lower-income classes have higher average and marginal propensities to consume housing services and thus they bear a greater proportion of 'shifted' property taxes.

If ability to pay were measured with greater regard for wealth, and if consistent assumptions regarding 'shifting' were maintained for all types of property taxes, then, as we have argued, it would seem likely that property taxes would be found to be less regressive than earlier studies concluded. This finding is quite consistent with analyses which stress that property taxes are similar to a benefit levy for financing state and local government expenditures on property-oriented services. This result is also quite consistent with our normative judgment

---

1. James M. Buchanan, *The public finances*, Homewood (Illinois), Irwin, 1960 (pp. 461-462).

that local, and in part state, taxes should be benefit-oriented and the income redistribution should be left to the federal tax structure.

Although governments have employed the property tax base for centuries, they have seldom done so either consistently among themselves or uniformly through time. Tax assessors are poorly informed generally and tax administration is subject to powerful political pressures throughout the states. Prevailing property tax assessment procedures tend to make the rates proportionately higher for lower price property than for more expensive property; higher for newly developed than for old property; and higher for business property (especially large firms) than for property of individual citizens.

In recent years, a number of studies have been made to estimate the income elasticity of this tax. As Dick Netzer points out:

'The concept of income elasticity... is rather more ambiguous for the property tax than for most other taxes.... First, the nominal or legal base of the tax — assessed values — and the economic base of the tax — the market value of taxable property — do not necessarily vary proportionately with one another. Second, local government jurisdictions typically can adjust both the legal base (assessments) and nominal tax rates, an option not present with other taxes. Third, actual property tax revenues are residually determined for most local governments: the tax levy equals previously determined expenditures less revenues from other sources, notably state aid. Thus, the elasticity of property tax revenue is really a reflection of the income elasticity of the demand for local government expenditure (or of residual revenue needs).'[1]

Robert Lampman estimated the income elasticity of the property tax to be 1.2 and concluded that the high elasticity of the recent past might be continued.[2]

Eugene McLoone, using national wealth estimates prepared by Raymond Goldsmith, concentrated on the real property tax base and concluded that the income elasticity has approached 1 over the years, and that a coefficient of 0.8 is the most reasonable one to use in projections for the years immediately ahead.[3] McLoone estimated that the income elasticity of property taxes in agricultural taxing districts throughout the nation averages 0.5, that non-farm business property taxes have a long-term elasticity of 0.57 and that the income elasticity of personal property taxes is 1.2. Using early 1960 data, McLoone estimated that state-by-state property tax elasticity coefficients vary from a low of 0.47 to a high of 1.08.

In the mid-sixties a large-scale effort was undertaken under the direction of Selma Mushkin to project state and local taxes for 1970. Projected changes in the yields of the present tax structure, aggregated geographically for each tax, were related to the assumed changes in gross national product on which

---

1. Dick Netzer, *Economics of the property tax*, Washington D.C., Brookings, 1966 (p. 185).
2. Robert J. Lampman, 'How much government spending in the 1960's ?' in *Quarterly review of economics and business*, Urbana (Illinois), Bureau of Economic and Business Research, Vol. II, February 1961.
3. Eugene P. McLoone, 'The facts of tax elasticity and financial support of education', (Ph.D. dissertation, University of Illinois, 1961).

the projections were based. These elasticities generally agree with earlier findings but there are considerable state-to-state variations. Property tax elasticities were estimated on two assumptions: firstly, that the property tax base grows with the market value of property and that the ratios of assessments to market values of property remain unchanged; and secondly, that the rate of time-lag in reassessment observable between 1956 and 1961 will continue. Under the first assumption property tax elasticity, averaged for all states, turned out to be 1.2 with respect to changes in gross national product and 1.3 with respect to changes in personal income. Under the second assumption the elasticities turned out to be 1 and 1.1 respectively.[1]

School property taxes

The one overriding fact about local school revenue is that the school district is dependent primarily on the property tax for local school support. Even in the total state/local partnership the local property tax provides, on the average, more than half of the revenue supporting public education. The percentages of support vary greatly from state to state, with Iowa, New Hampshire, and Nebraska providing more than 80 per cent of their state/local revenue from the local property tax, while Delaware secures less than 20 per cent from this source. Moreover, the differences between districts within a state are marked.

A second significant fact about the property tax in relation to school support is that this tax is shared with other local governmental units. This sharing frequently leads to intense competition for the tax dollar. Often the school district by itself is not in a position to decree the extent to which the property base may be utilized to provide school district revenue.

Schools have managed to increase their claim on the property tax. Between 1942 and 1969 the portion devoted to schools rose from about one-third to slightly more than one-half (see Figure 1). During this period, schools displaced both cities and counties as the major recipients of property tax revenue.

In summary, the property tax has been a highly productive revenue source throughout the post-World War II period. However, since the late 1960s it has appeared to be running into serious difficulties. These might stem from some of its major shortcomings: the property tax as the source of local school support does not relate well to the ability to pay or to the benefits received. Also, it overburdens some individuals and property owners, particularly the aged and the low-income groups.[2] A final criticism relates to the inadequacy of its administration and the horizontal overlap of tax jurisdictions.

1. Selma Mushkin, *Property taxes: 1970 outlook*, Chicago, Council of State Governments, 1965 (p. 23).
2. Wisconsin and Minnesota have pioneered in the use of an income tax/credit tax rebate 'circuit breaker' technique to protect individuals and families from extreme property tax burdens. Advisory Commission on Intergovernmental Relations, *Fiscal balance in the American federal system*, Washington, D.C., 1967 (Vol. 1, p. A-31).

Financing public first-level and second-level education in the U.S.A.

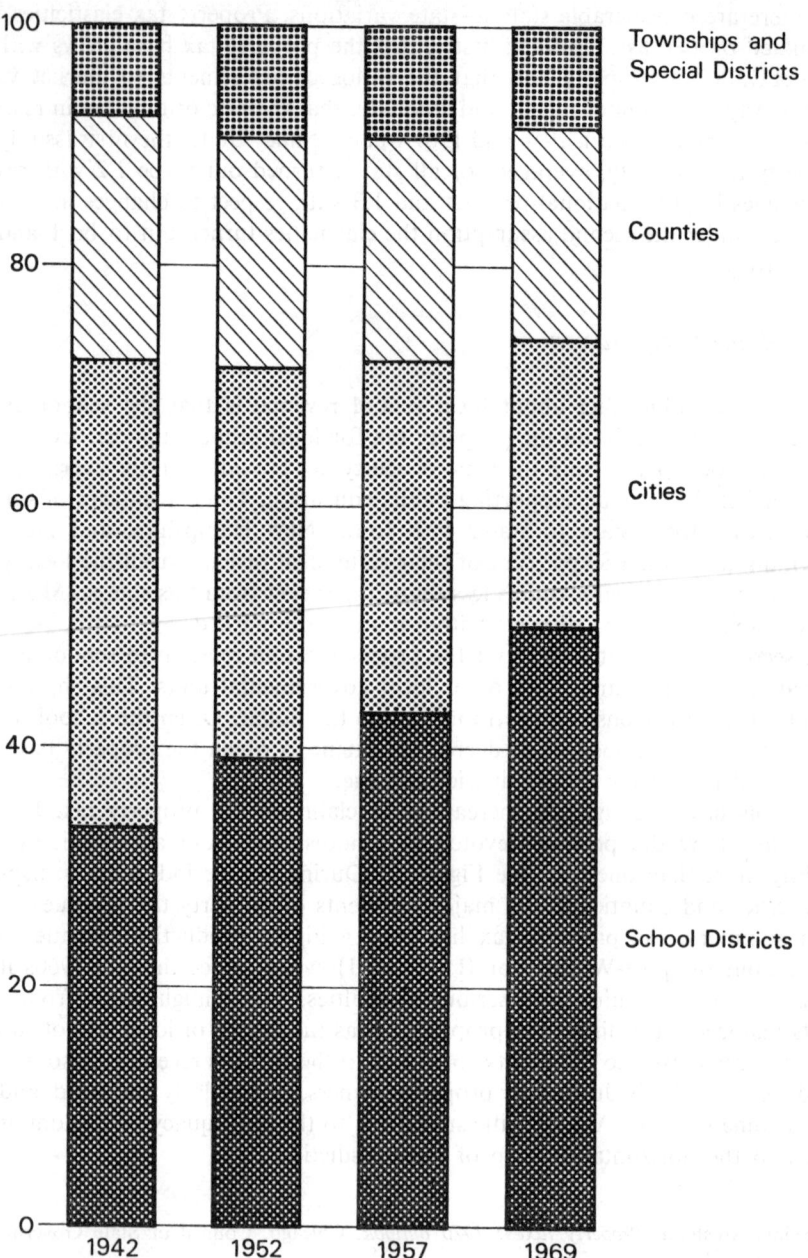

FIGURE 1. *Percentage distribution of local property tax collections, by type of government*
SOURCE *State aid to local governement,* op. cit., p. 37

Non-property taxes raised by local school districts

The first local non-property taxes were levied by cities rather than by school districts. New York city led with a tax on retail sales in 1934. Philadelphia followed with a sales tax, but substituted a flat rate income tax in 1939. The most sweeping provision for local non-property taxes was inaugurated by the state of Pennsylvania in 1947 when the legislature voted to permit local units of government, including school districts, to levy any tax not levied by the state. More than 2,000 school districts in Pennsylvania have levied some form of local non-property tax.

Burkhead has summarized the status of local non-property taxes levied by local units of government:

'Although the aggregate of local non-property tax revenue stabilized at about 12 or 13 per cent of local tax collections in the decade of the 1950s, this development has been significantly important in some states. In seventeen states in 1960, local nonproperty taxes were less than 5 per cent of total local taxes, but in New York State they were 23 per cent of the total; in Pennsylvania, 25.9 per cent; and in Alabama (local sales taxes) they were 43.7 per cent. Moreover, these levies are important for cities with population of more than 1,000,000. With the recent addition of Detroit, all of the nation's five largest cities now have local non-property levies.'[1]

Municipalities have been authorized to use local non-property taxes more frequently than have school districts. This does not preclude some indirect assistance to school districts, however, as some leeway may be produced by the municipalities receiving revenue from non-property taxes which would otherwise have to come from the property tax. Presumably a greater portion of property tax income may then go to the school district.

The duplication of taxes already being levied is an important argument against local non-property taxes. Those taxes producing greatest revenue have usually been preempted by either the federal or state levels of government. In many states, taxpayers already pay federal and state income taxes. To add a payroll tax brings cries of anguish that double taxation has now been stretched to triple taxation. The annoyance of a multiplicity of taxes scores heavily against non-property taxes.

The proponents of local non-property taxes point out that these taxes do bring additional tax revenues not otherwise available to school districts and that these revenues either buttress the property tax or, where rates are unduly high, bring tax relief. Most of the non-property taxes respond more quickly than property taxes to changes in the economic welfare of the country; they bring responsiveness and flexibility to the local tax picture.

---

1. Jesse Burkhead, *State and local taxes for public education*, Syracuse, Syracuse University Press, 1963 (pp. 99-100).

IV. Intergovernmental fiscal relations

Because of widespread spatial spillovers of education costs and benefits, equity considerations related to the merit good aspects of education, and the reliance of school districts on property- and not people-oriented services, financial support from higher levels of government is justified and needed. Furthermore, states stipulate by law many school activities that are to be carried out by districts, for which the state, logically, should pay. For example, in the case of California the mandated programmes seem to dominate all others by far.

State and federal governments have recognized this condition and, in general, since World War II have greatly increased their support to local governments, as shown in Section II. We will next take a general look at intergovernmental instruments before examining specific state and federal programmes in later sections.

Intergovernmental fiscal instruments

The techniques by which state and federal governments can fund school district activities may be divided into at least two major categories: direct transfer of funds, and sharing of the tax revenues of state and federal governments with school districts by indirect transfers. Categorical grants and unrestricted grants fall into the first classification, and tax supplements and tax allowances into the second.

CATEGORICAL GRANTS

Categorical grants are money transfers to subordinate governments made without conditions of repayment, but exchanged for stipulated spending commitments that are binding on the subordinate governments. Categorical grants differ as to the restrictions imposed on the use of grant funds in such qualification criteria as different matching requirements. The donor can apply different formulas for the distribution of funds.

In the past, categorical grants have been heavily relied upon and their importance has continued to increase. Spillover and distributive considerations favour state and federal aid to specific school programmes, since national values and goals can be pursued in this manner. Categorical grants enable the state and federal governments to maintain control over the expenditures of schools, greatly increasing the chance that programmes considered important to the national interest are initiated and carried out. Thus, categorical grants can increase economic efficiency by compensating for spatial spillovers of benefits and costs and reducing regional inequalities in services and income, even though they inhibit local initiative and responsibility.

UNRESTRICTED GRANTS

Unrestricted or block grants appeal to school officials who fear that categorical grants increase the concentration of power in state or federal governments. By providing unrestricted grants, state and federal governments express their confidence that schools are competent to decide what services should be provided, and to whom, as well as to render those educational services effectively and in the most desirable quantities.

Block grants in general avoid certain of the shortcomings of categorical grants. But block grants pose some serious problems concerning the redistribution of income between school districts and individuals: the possible adverse effects on the state's tax effort, the desire of the states to provide a pass-through of federal funds, and the danger that schools will allocate funds to expenditures that in the view of the state or federal government have low priority.

Of the second type of intergovernmental fiscal instruments, i.e. sharing of state and federal government tax revenues with school districts by indirect ransfers, we will consider here only tax supplements and tax allowances.

TAX SUPPLEMENTS

A school district, if it is legally authorized to do so, can participate in a tax supplement plan by applying its own tax rate to a tax base defined by the state government. The school tax, collected by the state together with its own tax on that tax base, is transferred to the district, which simply pays for the collection service. The district remains free to vary its tax rate each year according to its financial needs. The taxpayer files a single state tax return, and perhaps is unaware that he is paying a school tax.

TAX ALLOWANCES — DEDUCTIONS AND CREDITS

Subordinate government tax allowances are provisions in the tax laws of higher levels of government that give special treatment to persons who paid certain taxes to the subordinate governments. These special allowances permit subordinate governments to share indirectly the tax base of the higher level of government. For example, existing laws make it possible for taxpayers to avoid some federal income tax by making payments to subordinate governments, including school districts. The federal government determines which subordinate government taxes will be sanctioned for special treatment and how much the allowance will be. One form of allowance is termed 'deductibility' and allows federal (or state) income taxpayers to reduce gross taxable income by the amount of sanctioned payments. The second form of allowance is termed 'crediting' and allows income taxpayers to reduce their federal (or state) tax liability by the amount of sanctioned payment to subordinate governments.

Existing deductions permit taxpayers to reduce their taxable income for federal income tax purposes, with school district and state taxes qualifying for this deduction. Tax credit provisions allow certain state and school tax payments to be credited against federal income tax liability, in part or in full. Tax credits and tax deductions represent a highly flexible fiscal device which can be used by federal and state governments to prevent taxation of the same base by the federal, state and local governments, and thus they can be used to increase the fiscal power of state and local governments.

In view of the opposition of local taxpayers to increases in school taxes, will they accept federal or state deductions as a means of reducing their burden of marginal local tax increases? Although there are no easy answers to this question, it appears that taxpayers do consider deductibility when making tax decisions.[1] There is some evidence that tax credits tend to be more effective than tax deductions; the difference in effectiveness is one of degree. In general and under similar circumstances, tax credits tend to produce greater savings to taxpayers than tax deductions. Tax credits should therefore offer taxpayers and legislators greater incentive to qualify for federal or state tax savings by instituting or raising local taxes that can be offset against the federal or state taxes.

---

1. See Werner Z. Hirsch, *The economics of state and local government*, New York, McGraw-Hill, 1970 (p. 125).

V. State support for schools

Of the various intergovernmental fiscal instruments, state grants-in-aid are by far the most important to education in the United States. For example in 1967 state grants to education amounted to $11.8 thousand million, i.e. about 42 per cent of the revenue receipts of school districts.

We will present below a number of methods for distributing school aid that give varying patterns to the educational demand resources, and tax efforts of school districts.

Flat grants

A flat grant is usually tied to the number of students enrolled in a district. As more pupils raise the financial needs of the district, the state responds with a fixed sum based on the teacher salary schedule and pupil unit measures.

Delaware, which operates on this system, refines its measure of need further by distinguishing pupils on the basis of first and second level grades and mental or physical handicaps. Delaware does not require a minimum local effort and therefore ignores any disparity in local resources and tax effort. Although this might be a flaw under certain conditions, it may not be in Delaware's case because of that state's heavy reliance on personal income tax. Where the flat grant represents a high proportion of total cost — 65.8 per cent in Delaware in 1966 — and where the districts are few in number — fifty-one in Delaware — and similar in local resources, the flat grant plan may nonetheless result in a fairly equalized dollar support for public schools.[1]

Flat grants in conjunction with categorical aid

Some states, e.g. North Carolina and Connecticut, have enacted combination plans.[2] The evaluation of the North Carolina system parallels that for Delaware,

---

1. *State aid to local government*, op. cit., p. 42.
2. North Carolina pays the total calculated amount for salaries, transportation, and associated school costs of a basic programme. Expenditures in excess of the state programme are permitted but are a local obligation. In addition, there is state aid for such categories as vocational education, driving school, school lunches, professional improvement and educational TV.

except that categorical aid tends to reward the wealthy districts for effort they can more easily make. The latter point takes on increased significance in Connecticut for two reasons: the state government finances a smaller share of the total school spending (31 per cent) and therefore equalization becomes more essential; and, the number of categories — twenty in all — begins to outrun the administrative capacity of local officials.

Matching grants

In the hope of stimulating local financial efforts, usually to finance specific programmes, some states provide grants that require the addition of local funds. One of the more popular programmes financed in this way is school construction. Thus state formulas offer matching funds in a fixed ratio: e.g., Delaware, 60 per cent state/40 per cent local; Florida, 50 per cent state/50 per cent local. There is an incentive to spend local funds, but wealthy districts can respond more easily than poor ones. If there are appreciable differences in resources or efforts among districts, the wealthy soon outstrip the poor districts in construction and replacement of school facilities. Matching grants, however, do serve well as a means of getting new activities started.

Equalization grants

Equalization grants are offered by states on the theory that aid to a local district should bear an inverse relationship to the resources of that district. For example, the ratio of state to local funds might be set at $1 for every $7 for the wealthiest district while for the poorest district it might be the reverse, or $7 of state funds for each $1 of local funds.

This is the underlying rationale for the so-called 'foundation-type' state aid that dominates the public school financing picture. Frequently a ceiling specifies the amount beyond which the state no longer matches local funds. This ceiling prevents strict equalization. Rhode Island and Wisconsin come closest to equalization without limit; no ceiling is placed on the amount of state support available on a matching basis, and state funds compensate for local resource disparities under a so-called 'equalized percentage matching grant'.

Two basic fiscal features of the foundation programme are the local rate and the measure of relative tax paying capacity. In most states the measure of capacity is equalized property value. However in a few states, mostly in the south, a proxy for property value is constructed from various local measures of income and wealth.[1]

---

1. Utah treats the required local contribution in a unique manner. Under the provisions of its foundation programme, all school districts are required to levy a property tax of 16 *mills* on the state-equalized fair value of taxable property in the district. This levy is mandatory and local receipts produced by it in excess of $7,250 per distribution unit (twenty-seven pupils) plus the amount allowed for pupil transportation expenses are collected as a state tax and used for foundation programme support in other districts rather than being retained

What is the pattern of current state aid ? If we separate state aid into non-categorical and categorical aid, in 1966/67 the first type covered about 85 per cent of all aid and the remaining 15 per cent was earmarked for transportation, textbooks, etc.[1] Of the non-categorical aid about three-quarters was accounted for by equalizing grants, (at the same time they accounted for only 30 per cent of categorical aid).

Since the early 1950s the pattern of state aid has undergone change both in method and in purpose. These developments are summarized in Table 8.

States differ in the manner in which state aid is distributed — flat versus equalizing — reflecting major differences in the state/local sharing of financial

TABLE 8. Estimated amount and percentage of state grants distributed for public school purposes, by purpose and method of distribution. selected years. ($ million)

Purpose and method of distribution	1953/54	1957/58	1962/63 [1]	1966/67
All purposes	2 980	4 516	6 539	9 645
Flat	1 572	1 892	2 506	2 970
Equalizing	1 408	2 625	4 033	6 675
General purpose	2 407	3 712	5 806	8 174
Flat	1 185	1 386	2 027	1 928
Equalizing	1 222	2 326	3 779	6 246
Special purpose	573	815	733	1 471
Flat	388	576	479	1 042
Equalizing	185	299	254	429
		Percentage distribution		
All purposes	100.0	100.0	100.0	100.0
Flat	52.8	41.9	38.3	30.8
Equalizing	47.2	58.2	61.7	69.2
General purpose	80.8	82.2	88.8	84.7
Flat	39.8	30.7	31.0	20.0
Equalizing	41.0	51.5	57.8	64.7
Special purpose	19.2	18.0	11.2	15.3
Flat	13.0	11.4	7.3	10.8
Equalizing	6.2	6.6	3.9	4.4

1. Not including Tennessee where about $120 million of state grants were predominantly for general purposes and distributed on an equalizing basis.
SOURCE Office of Education, *State programs of public school support*, Washington, D.C., U.S. Department of Health, Education and Welfare.

in the district of origin. No other state comes as close as this in the imposition of a uniform state tax rate for school support. Excess local levies in other states are retained locally to supplement the foundation programme.

Michigan, too, treats the tax rate and capacity factors uniquely. Local districts with overall local levies on state equalized values of 125 per cent or more above the levies in other districts have their state equalized value for foundation programme purposes reduced proportionately.

1. *State aid to local government*, op. cit., p. 40.

responsibilities. Delaware, New Mexico, and North Carolina provide flat grants to cover current expenditure per pupil. Localities have the authority to (and do) supplement the state minimum support level by imposing a local property tax rate for schools. No state aid dollars are devoted to equalizing the burden of the locally obtained supplements. Nonetheless, only thirteen states used the flat grant method to distribute at least 50 per cent or more of state aid in 1966/67, including the five that used this method exclusively or almost exclusively (Figure 2).[1]

The majority of states favour the equalizing grant method to distribute the bulk of school aid. Every state aid dollar in Rhode Island equalizes. More than $90 of every $100 of state aid equalizes in Georgia, Idaho, Kentucky, Maine, Michigan, Nevada, New York, Ohio, Tennessee, and Utah. Indiana and South Carolina spell out how a major portion of state school aid must be spent. In South Carolina, the state specifies the budget categories on all of its aid to local schools. Wyoming, Idaho, New York, and Ohio, in contrast, delegate to local school officials all budget decisions.

Details on grant programmes in two states

As we have seen above, state aid programmes are very complicated and differ greatly between states. We will present in detail two state grant programmes as examples: California, with its extensively-developed system of school grants based mainly on the fixed-unit equalizing concept; and Rhode Island with its recently-instituted, open-ended, percentage equalizing grant systems.

CALIFORNIA

In population, California is the largest state of the United States, having a 1970 population in excess of twenty million. It has more than 1,200 school districts. School revenue in 1968/69 amounted to $3.7 thousand million (60 per cent locally-raised, 34 per cent state aid, and 6 per cent federal aid).[2] The grant programme of California is well described by Charles Benson.[3]

'In 1966/67 California employed not one but three fixed-unit equalization grants. For elementary schools the foundation program was defined as $249 per unit of average daily attendance. The local contribution rate was 60 cents per $100 of adjusted assessed valuation. (The valuation was adjusted on two counts: to establish intercounty equalization of property values and to capitalize into the valuation a portion of federal grants for impacted areas and of other miscellaneous receipts). For high school attendance, the foundation program was $339, with a local contribution rate of 50 cents per $100 of adjusted valuation. The grant for junior colleges had a foundation program of $600 and

---

1. *State aid to local government*, op. cit., pp. 41-42.
2. Advisory Commission on Intergovernmental Relations, *State and local finances*, Washington, D.C., 1969 (M-50, pp. 46, 57).
3. Charles S. Benson, *The economics of public education*, Boston, Houghton Mifflin, 1968 (2nd ed., pp. 186-188).

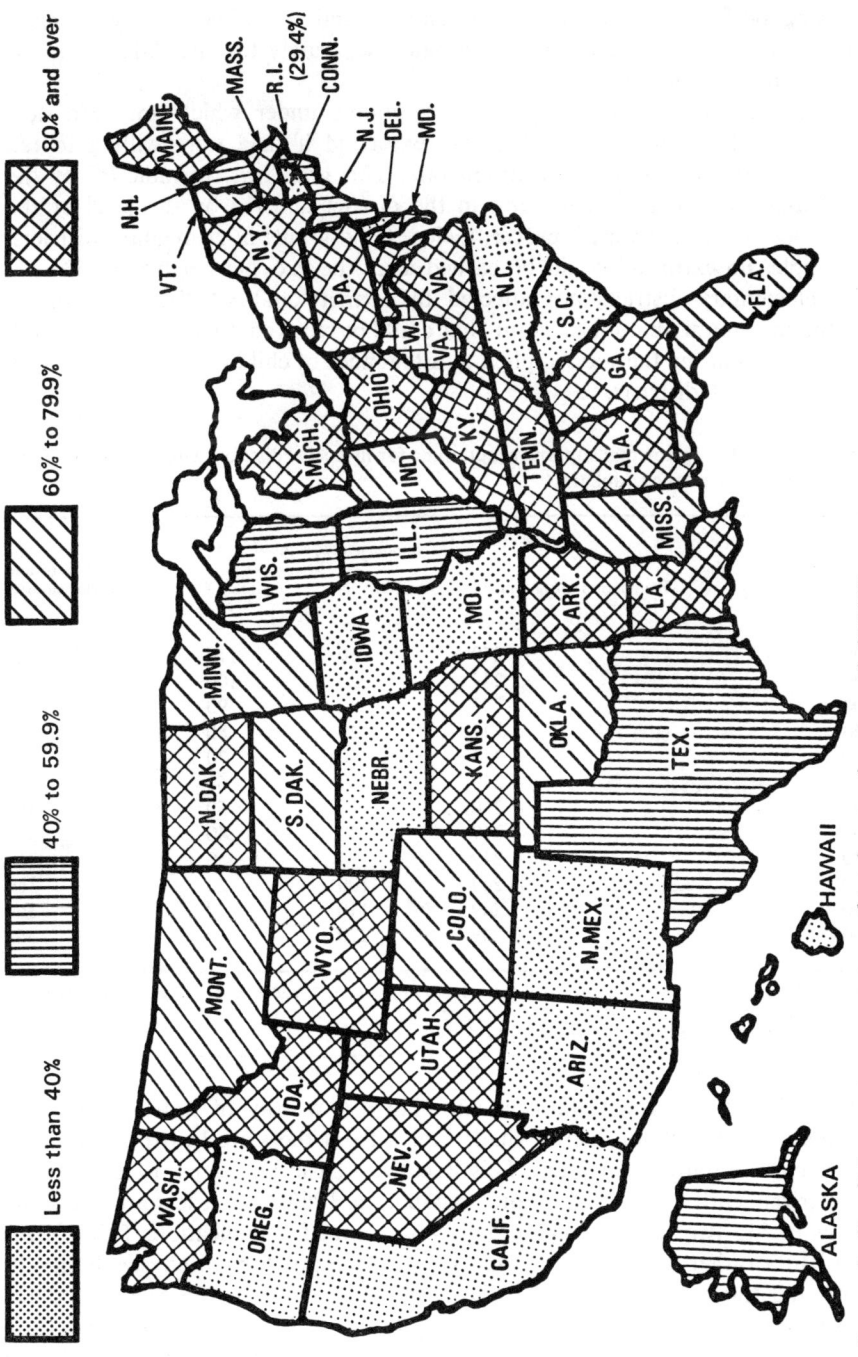

FIGURE 2. *Equalizing grants as percentage of total state education aid, 1966/67*
SOURCE *State aid to local government*, op. cit., p. 41

a local contribution rate of 25 cents. Even for "unified districts", i.e., those comprising both elementary and high schools (and sometimes junior colleges, as well), the grant entitlement was computed separately for the different levels of school attendance.

'In addition, there were supplementary grants, under which approximately the poorer half of districts could obtain extra aid if they were willing to tax themselves above the local contribution rate. This grant was variable (a) by the level of assessed valuation per pupil in the district and (b) by the level of the local school tax rate. It was, however, a closed-end grant; in elementary districts, for example, no extra aid could be earned after the tax rate reached $1.60.

'For elementary districts not affected by sparsity and small-school corrections, the maximum amount of grant that could be received is shown in Table [9]. The same amount, by the way, applied to attendance of children in the elementary grades of unified districts.

TABLE 9. Present supplemental support programme for first-level districts with over 900 average daily attendance (dollars)

Assessed valuation per unit of ADA	Foundation programme [1]	Supplemental support		Total state and district support
		District	State [2]	
1 000	249	10	110	369
2 000	249	20	100	369
3 000	249	30	90	369
4 000	249	40	80	369
5 000	249	50	70	369
6 000	249	60	60	369
7 000	249	70	50	369
8 000	249	80	40	369
9 000	249	90	30	369
10 000	249	100	20	369
11 000	249	110	10	369
12 000	249	120	0	369

1. Does not include $20 per unit of average daily attendance in grades 1, 2, and 3 to meet class size standards.
2. Assumes tax rate of $1.60 or more.
SOURCE *The economics of public education*, op. cit., p. 187.

'Other features of the California aid plan are worthy of note. First, it is stipulated that no school district shall receive from the state less than $125 per unit of average daily attendance. This is called "basic aid", and it is what we characterized earlier as a flat grant. Second, in 1966/67 districts were offered a bonus of $15 per unit of average daily attendance for unification. Third, California had a rather detailed set of excess expense grants for the physically handicapped and the mentally retarded. Districts were eligible to be reimbursed for 100 per cent of the excess expense of schooling for these children, up to certain maximum limits (in 1966/67, for example, $910 for physically handicapped minors). Fourth, the state provides a system of bonuses and penalties (quite severe penalties actually) to promote the progressive reduction of class size in grades 1, 2, and 3. Fifth, the state offers districts a rather unique form of "aid in kind", namely, the services of specially selected reading teachers who are available to work full time in the instruction of pupils in grades 1-3, under the operational objective of minimizing reading failure at the fourth grade level. Sixth, school districts in California, unlike most municipal governments, operate under strict local property tax rate limits. This situation has become confused, however, because of the large number of "permissive overrides" on functionally defined exceptions to the limits that have been passed by the legislature.

'Certain claims can be made for California school support. An enormous influx of population has been accommodated without resort to such economy devices as double sessions. California teachers' salaries are generally the highest in the nation. The state, as we noted earlier, has developed a magnificent system of public higher education.

'But there are also shortcomings, more or less predictable in nature. First, a considerable variation exists among districts in expenditure per pupil and there is no evidence that these differences are so arranged that educational output of the state is maximized. Interdistrict tax rate differentials are substantial; in 1965/66, school tax rates varied from a low of $1.27 per $100 of assessed valuation to a high of $7. In spite of the equalizing features of the state aid plan, the revenue potentials of districts (per pupil) at a given tax rate show large differences, as Table 10 indicates.

'Second, though the legislature has seen fit to revise the amounts of the foundation program upward at frequent intervals, a substantial volume of the additional school aid is dissipated in tax relief and flows over into the support of other local government services. A recent study of this problem reported the following: " ... it is concluded that of the 1952/53 changes in California state aid to education only approximately 20 per cent went to increase total educational expenditures beyond what they would have been if there had been no change in state aid. More than 65 per cent of the change in state aid was employed by local government to reduce their local tax burdens, and somewhat less than 15 per cent was shifted to the financing of other local government services ".[1]

' Third, the large cities of the state feel they are receiving insufficient funds in view of the costs of education in high-density areas.[2] This complaint, of course, is by no means peculiar to California, though some states, like New York, have been quicker to respond to it. (In New York in 1966/67 the large cities received a 20 per cent bonus on state aid as otherwise computed.)'[3]

1. John T. Rowntree, Jr., 'The efficiency of intergovernmental grants', (Ph.D. dissertation, University of California, Berkeley, 1966), p. 90.
2. Rafferty, Cox and Johnson, *Recommendations on public school support*, Sacramento, California State Department of Education, 1967.
3. Nonetheless, the 1967 California legislature did make a number of changes in the details of the state aid programme. Foundation programme amounts, local contribution rates, limits on the amount of expense reimbursable in the handicapped programme, and the unification bonus were all increased.

TABLE 10. Support available per unit of average daily attendance (ADA) when tax rate is $1.60 (first level in dollars)

	Assessed valuation per unit of ADA		
	Low	Average	High
Type of support	Baldwin Park Unified $4 824	Downey Unified $13 382	Beverly Hills Unified $81 661
State			
Basic aid	125.00	125.00	125.00
Equalization aid	116.06	64.71	—
Supplemental support	71.76	—	—
Local			
Tax rate, $1.60	77.18	214.11	1 306.58
TOTAL	390.00	403.82	1 431.58

SOURCE *The economics of public education*, op. cit., p. 188.

RHODE ISLAND

Unlike California, the state of Rhode Island is one of the smaller of the United States, with forty school districts in 1966. School revenue in 1968/69 amounted to $125 million, with 58 per cent locally-raised, 35 per cent state aid, and 7 per cent federal aid.[1]

Charles Benson also well describes the Rhode Island grant programme:[2]

'Rhode Island distributes both its general aid and its funds in support of school construction under the percentage equalizing formula $A_i = (1 - 0.7875 \frac{y_i}{y}) E_i$.

Where A_i = grant to district i;
y_i = assessed valuation per pupil in the district;
y = assessed valuation per pupil in the state;
E_i = school expenditure in district i.

'Rhode Island has no categorical aids in the conventional sense and no mandated property tax limits. The state shares without limit in the locally determined levels of expenditure. That is, the Rhode Island plan is truly open-ended. Practically any kind of expenditure legally authorized by a local school committee is eligible for reimbursement. With minor changes the plan has been in effect since 1960/61.

'From the introduction of the plan to the year 1964/65, state aid rose from $9,341,000 to $24,122,000, an increase of 158.2 per cent. This was far ahead

1. *State and local finances*, op. cit., p. 45.
2. *The economics of public education*, op. cit., pp. 188-190.

of the national average rise — 51.2 per cent — in state aid during these years. However, because the plan when introduced was considerably more generous than the fixed-unit plan it replaced and because of an upward revision in the overall state share made in 1963/64, it has been possible for the rises in state aid to overshadow increases in local expenditure. In 1959/60, the last year of the old grants, current expenditure in Rhode Island was $399 per pupil, 6.4 per cent above national average; in 1964/65, expenditure per pupil in Rhode Island was $520, but this figure was only 7.4 per cent above the national average. During the years when the percentage equalizing plan has been in effect, then, there has been only a slight improvement in Rhode Island's expenditure position, in spite of a vast increase in state aid. The grant's expected effect in stimulating local expenditures has not materialized.

'Moreover, a recent study of the experience with this new type of grant indicates that the geographical flow of funds has favoured the high-income, suburban district, not the older industrial cities.[1] That is, it is the suburban districts that have been quickest to raise their local expenditure and draw extra aid.

'In spite of the flexibility inherent in the Rhode Island school finance plan, the functional allocation of funds within districts appears to have held remarkably constant, as Table [11] shows. Such stability is itself a matter of concern.

[There is a] lack of clear evidence that the opportunity provided by the open-ended matching grant to extend school services into relatively neglected, but socially crucial, areas has been seized. Table [11] indicated that expen-

TABLE 11. Percentage shares of total current expenditures by function or purpose, Rhode Island, 1959/60 and 1964/65

Function or object	Share 1959/60	Share 1964/65	Change in percentage points
General control	2.9	2.8	−0.1
Instruction	71.3	70.4	−0.9
Operation of plant	10.1	9.3	−0.8
Maintenance of plant	3.5	3.0	−0.5
Fixed charges	2.7	5.1	+2.4
Auxiliary services	8.3	7.8	−0.5
Evening schools	0.2	0.2	0.0
Summer schools	0.1	0.1	0.0
Capital outlay for current revenue	0.8	1.2	+0.4
TOTAL	100.0	100.0	

SOURCE *The economics of public education*, op. cit., p. 190.

1. Charles S. Benson and James A. Kelly, *The Rhode Island comprehensive foundation and enhancement state aid program for education*, Providence, Rhode Island Special Commission to Study the Entire Field of Education, 1966 (p. 17). The Rhode Island law has since been modified to afford somewhat more preferential treatment to the large cities.

ditures on summer schools and evening schools has remained minuscule; the increase in provision was exactly *pro rata* with the change in total current expenditures in Rhode Island. Local expenditures on vocational schools rose by only $97,000 in the 5-year period and in 1964/65 remained below half a million. Kindergarten enrollment increased by only 467 in five years and in 1964/65 remained below 10,000.[1] There is no specific entry on Form 31 [the expenditure reporting form] to show expenditures on the retraining of teachers; examination of entries in the various "other expenditure" categories indicates, however, that very small sums have been spent on in-service programs in the schools. It is the stability of the pattern of Rhode Island's expenditures in the face of profound social change that is worrisome.[2]

'In summary, though both the California and Rhode Island school finance plans are carefully—and we might say imaginatively—designed, they offer results that in various respects are disappointing. Our conclusion is that the structure of the system of finance, though that structure has been of such major interest to school administrators since the early 1920s, is itself not the important determinant of educational progress in a state. Of possibly much greater importance is the quality of leadership offered in the state government. The educational interest groups might well shift their attention from the design and revision of state aid programs to such matters as the definition and costing of operational objectives in education and to efforts to convince the local authorities that they should make serious efforts to fulfill the agreed-upon objectives. The resulting financial requirements in the different districts could then be computed rather easily, it would seem.'

---

1. The increase in kindergarten enrolment over the five years fell short of the increase in the number of 5-year-old children in the state by over 450.
2. Benson and Kelly, op. cit., p. 26.

VI. Federal support for schools

Among the various states there are large income differences, even if measured on a *per capita* basis. In the immediate post-World War II period, e.g. in 1958, the unweighted mean income *per capita* of the five richest states was $1,760, or about 94 per cent higher than that of the lowest five, with $908. About twenty years later the differential had declined somewhat to about 75 per cent. Thus, children living in poorer states in the United States, without federal intervention, tend to have a lesser opportunity for a good education than children living in the richer states. This assertion is borne out by the existence of a very high correlation between personal income and public school expenditures in the different states. For example, Charles Benson has found that in 1966 61 per cent of the variation in expenditure per public school pupil could be explained on the average in terms of *per capita* personal income.[1] Thus, it is the responsibility of the federal government to participate in the financing of local schools in a manner that helps equalize educational opportunity, be it in terms of input or output.

In addition to seeking an equalization of educational opportunity, the federal government in the past has seen fit to finance local schools with a view to attaining specific goals deemed in the national interest. Historically, as a matter of fact, most federal funds went for such purposes. A third type of federal financial programme has been in existence for some time and is designed to compensate local school districts for revenue losses that might occur when tax-exempt federal installations are located in their areas.

In order to give federal financial aid to education a historical perspective, we will start with the Vocational Education Act, offering aid for the attainment of specified national goals, then turn to impact laws designed to reimburse local schools for tax losses resulting from tax exempt federal installations, and finally to recent laws designed to increase—sometimes in a *sub rosa* manner—equality of educational opportunity.

---

1. *The economics of public education*, op. cit., pp. 193-194.

Vocational Education Act

In 1917 the United States Congress passed the Smith-Hughes Act designed to stimulate vocational education, both because such education had been neglected and because of labour shortages. The act provided continuing appropriations, initially $6 million a year, in support of salaries of teachers of agriculture, home economics, trade and industry, and distributive occupations. The George-Barden Act of 1946 authorized additional annual appropriations of $29 million for training in the four vocational education fields mentioned. Grants are allocated to the states on the basis of population; in the case of agricultural education, rural population is the basis, and in the case of trade and industry, urban population is the basis. States or localities must match these federal funds dollar-for-dollar.

Title VIII of the National Defense Education Act of 1958 appropriated an additional $15 million for vocational schools to turn out highly skilled technicians. The Vocational Education Act of 1963 provided the permanent authorization for federal appropriations of $225 million annually and a 1967/68 temporary authorization of $35 million. The objective of the 1963 act had income redistribution overtones since it provided for occupational training for persons who have completed or left high school and are seeking the opportunity to obtain occupational training. The act extended the occupational fields in which federal funds could be used in support of training programmes and provided money for the construction of local or regional vocational schools.

Altogether it appears that the Vocational Education Act has been successful in stimulating state and local governments to find training programmes. Less than $3 million were spent on vocational education by all levels of government in 1917; forty-six years later expenditures were $333 million. Federal funds are overmatched by both state and local expenditures, taken separately.[1] Hardly would such progress have been possible without federal leadership and financial incentive. Criticism of federal vocational aid has been in terms of the rigidity of controls under which the programme is carried out, and there are indications that in recent years federal controls have lessened and local responsibility has increased.

Science Education Acts

In addition to deciding that the United States needed more and better vocational training, Congress in the late 1950s decided, after being shocked by Russian successes in space, that the nation's security required fuller development of the mental resources and technical skills of its young. Initially aid was focused on improving instruction in mathematics, science, and foreign languages, together with improvement of guidance and counselling services. This was done through the National Defense Education Act of 1958. Successive legislative amendments

1. Bruce F. Davie and Philip D. Patterson, Jr., *Vocational education and intergovernmental fiscal relations in the postwar period*, Washington, D.C., Georgetown University, 1966 (p. 7).

(four by 1965) greatly enlarged the scope of support, providing today funds in support of instructional and auxiliary educational services of local school districts for certified personnel and teaching materials and equipment. School districts submit grant proposals and evidence for matching funds and are funded depending on the quality and acceptability of their plans. This programme, too, appears to have been successful in that each additional $1 per capita of federal education aid was associated, on the average among the states, with an increase in state local-school expenditures of more than $5 per capita. Criticism of this legislation has included claims that rich school districts with administrative and financial capability to participate in matching such categorical grants have been the principal beneficiaries, and that in the absence of mandated evaluation programmes the cost-effectiveness of these activities has not been proven.[1]

Federal Impact School Aid Acts

The laws discussed earlier, designed to help in the financing of vocational education and of education deemed desirable in relation to national defense, relied on categorical aid; a subsequent set of impact laws provides block grants for these purposes. The size of these block grants is substantial, amounting to about $500 million dollars per year in the late 1960s. In 1970 it was mainly these sizeable impact grants that produced a Presidential veto of the entire education appropriation, a veto that was sustained by Congress.

Impact aid is provided under PL874 and PL815, the first making grants available for current operating expenses of school districts, the second for school construction. Such aid is based on the premise that the federal government as a property-owner has the responsibility of a normal citizen in the community and owes financial support for local government services. However, federal property is exempt from local taxation and in lieu of paying property taxes the federal government should provide school districts with sums equivalent to the cost of educating federally-connected pupils—sums not received from the parents of those pupils. In principle the federal payment should make up the difference between local revenue per pupil collected from non-federally-connected residents and local revenue per pupil collected from federally-connected residents, times the number of federally-connected pupils of the district. Criticism of approach has centred on the fact that schools are favoured, because local government expenditures other than education are also incurred and not paid for by the federal government. Furthermore, the critics point to the fact that the Impact Act favours places where school expenditures are incurred and not places where the loss in tax revenue is felt.

Federal aid to equalize educational opportunity

As early as 1906 Ellwood P. Cubberley analyzed data from Massachusetts, Connecticut, Indiana, Washington, Kansas, California, Missouri, and Wisconsin,

---

1. David N. Evans and I.T. Johnson, *The impact in California of NDEA Titles III, VI, VIII*, Sacramento, California State Department of Education, 1967 (pp. 2-3).

and detected great inequalities in the quality of school programmes, incomes, and local tax loads. However, federal aid to equalize educational opportunities had to wait almost another sixty years.[1] Forty years after the publication of the Cubberley study, impetus was given to the drive for federal equalization funds by the late Senator Robert Taft. A leading figure in the Republican Party, Taft threw his prestige behind Senate Bill 181, 79th Congress, designed to provide federal money for teachers' salaries. In a speech to the United States Senate on August 1, 1946, Senator Taft reminded the Senate that, 'In general ... I have felt very strongly that education is a state and local responsibility. ... However, ... although they [many states] are devoting as much or more than the average amount, on the basis of their wealth and the current income spent on education by the entire nation, nevertheless they are unable to provide an adequate basic minimum education for their children, due to the great difference in income as between the states. ... So I feel that the federal government does have a responsibility to see that every child in the United States has at least a minimum education in order that each child may have the opportunity which lies at the very base of the whole system of our Republic.'[2] Nevertheless almost another twenty years passed before Congress enacted the Elementary and Secondary Education Act of 1965. This act provided in its first year almost $1.2 thousand million for Title I, the programme for the education of disadvantaged students. Under this title federal funds were to be distributed through the states to the local school districts on the basis of: (a) the count of children in the district living in families with an annual income of less than $2,000; and (b) the count of children living in families that receive more than $2,000 under the programme for aid to dependent children. The sum of these two figures was multiplied by one-half the average current expenditure per public school pupil in the state in the second preceding year, to establish the maximum grant for which a local school district was eligible. However, payments could not exceed 30 per cent of the current budget of any district. Title I of the 1965 Act channelled federal aid to poor states and to improve the schooling of poor children in wealthy states. The act thus equalized educational opportunity, allowing all states, regardless of wealth, to participate.

Funds distributed under Title I constituted categorical aid to specific target groups, i.e. the poor. The aid was not categorical by programme or type of resources purchased. The 1965 Act also attempted to concentrate sufficient funds in clearly targeted areas, and the average expenditure per student in its first year amounted to $119, although statewide average expenditures varied from $25 to $277.[3] Furthermore, the act mandated that different types of educational expenditures be evaluated, establishing for the first time by federal law the

---

1. Ellwood P. Cubberley, *School funds and their apportionment*, New York, Columbia University Teachers' College, 1906.
2. U.S. Congress, *Congressional record*, Washington, D.C., Government Printing Office, 1946 (Vol. 92, Part 8, p. 10620).
3. Office of Education, *First annual report, title I, elementary and secondary education act of 1965*, Washington, D.C., Government Printing Office, 1967 (p. IX).

need for auditing and evaluation of performance. Finally, the act established the principle that it is appropriate to spend markedly different amounts of money per pupil in different schools, even schools of the same grade level and within the same school district.

The other four titles of the Elementary and Secondary Act of 1965 provided an additional $220 million. One hundred million dollars was appropriated in 1965/66 under Title II for the acquisition of school library resources, textbooks, and other printed instructional material for the public and private first- and second-level schools. Title III set up a five-year programme for the development of new kinds of supplementary educational centres and the establishment of model school programmes. Title IV provided for the expansion of educational research, and Title V authorized a five-year programme designed to strengthen state educational agencies.

VII. Opportunities and prospects

In the United States during the post-World War II period we have seen advocacy of strong central government, in terms of both school district consolidation and emphasis on categorical grants from state and local governments. Recently a reverse trend has started, and government decentralization and block grants are being advocated. Arguments in favour of decentralization are related to an upsurge in a sense of alienation, powerlessness, and frustration on the part of many people, including a feeling that they as individuals cannot effectively register their preferences about decisions emanating from the government. However, decentralization, block grants, and local controls, if implemented, have built into them forces that tend to generate change. Providing more non-categorical grants and greater local influence on public programmes is likely to result in disparities in practice among the numerous school districts, brought on by differences in human and non-human resources. These disparities are likely to stimulate calls for central intervention to restore equality and balance, and thus the forces underlying categorical grants are likely to assert themselves again.

The United States is an exceedingly industrialized and urbanized country and its people are highly mobile; as a result, benefit and cost spillovers, particularly in relation to education, are widespread. Differences in regional income and education are quite large. In view of these conditions, a good case can be made for the federal government, and to some extent the state governments, assuming in years to come substantially greater responsibility for the financing of education. If the federal and state governments respond positively, they will want to have control over the use of 'their' funds.

At a time when incentives offered by higher levels of government for the sake of achieving national goals have again become popular, the basis of awards of categorical aid might shift from a need or opportunity basis to a performance or accountability basis. Such a change is particularly promising for education; the rising social costs of school failures (most of which are borne by local governments), together with sharply rising school expenditures unaccompanied by major productivity increases, have resulted in financial crisis. On the positive side, recent research is beginning to make it possible for us to know with some accuracy how to achieve specific educational outputs. For example, knowledge has been increasing about the frequency, duration, and intensity of particular educational activities needed to produce definite types of behaviour in students of different ages, aptitudes, and interests. As a result, our own analysis is reaching a stage where we can begin to determine cost-effective means to accomplish specific educational objectives. To the extent that it is possible to do so, state and federal funds allocated to educational improvement should take into account the specific service conditions associated with a given population; in this way some more nearly equal outputs in terms of learning will be produced. We have for a long time talked about equal opportunity for all in relation to first- and second-level education. But we have been slow to define 'equal opportunity'. Implicitly, we have looked upon equal opportunity in terms of providing for each child an equal amount of money for his first- and second-level education, or equal opportunity in terms of *inputs*. Rather, our concern should be to provide more nearly equal opportunity in terms of *output*.

While state and federal funds could be used to ensure minimum performance, educational improvement could be stimulated with the aid of state and/or federal matching grants. The cost of educational improvement should take into consideration the service conditions of the particular district, i.e. whether the same improvements might be more expensive to produce in one district than in another.

Finally, it must be recognized that the existing system of financial aid to local school districts is now being challenged in the courts. In a suit filed against the state of Michigan early in 1968, the Detroit School Board asserted that the system of financing public education in that state denied equal protection of the law to school children in its district. Since then, other suits have been filed in California, Illinois, Texas, and Virginia alleging violation of the Fourteenth Amendment of the United States Constitution and, in some instances, identical provisions in state constitutions.[1]

The court test cases are based on the assertion that children in poor urban and rural areas are provided with education vastly inferior to that provided in more favoured districts. This inequality in public education is the result of a system of financing that makes the accident of wealth or poverty the chief determinant of the availability of funds for public education in any locality. While it will take some time before these cases are decided, most likely in the highest court of the land, the fact that these lawsuits have been instituted may bring about revisions in state aid formulas. Specifically, larger expenditures in poor districts, in line with the Elementary and Secondary Education Act of 1965, are likely to result.

1. The Fourteenth Amendment to the United States Constitution states, among other things: 'No state shall make or enforce any law which shall abridge the privileges or the immunities of citizens of the United States; nor shall any state deprive any person of life, liberty, or property, without due process of law; nor deny to any person within its jurisdiction the equal protection of the laws.'

IIEP book list

The following books, published by Unesco: IIEP, are obtainable from the Institute or from Unesco and its national distributors throughout the world:

Educational cost analysis in action: case studies for planners (1972. Three volumes)

Educational development in Africa (1969. Three volumes, containing eleven African research monographs)

Educational planning: a bibliography (1964)

Educational planning: a directory of training and research institutions (1968)

Educational planning in the USSR (1968)

Financing educational systems (series of monographs: full list at front of this volume)

Fundamentals of educational planning (series of monographs: full list available on request)

Manpower aspects of educational planning (1968)

Methodologies of educational planning for developing countries by J.D. Chesswas (1968)

Monographies africaines (five titles, in French only: list available on request)

New educational media in action: case studies for planners (1967. Three volumes)

The new media: memo to educational planners by W. Schramm, P.H. Coombs, F. Kahnert, J. Lyle (1967. A report including analytical conclusions based on the above three volumes of case studies)

Planning the development of universities — I (1971. Further volumes to appear)

Population growth and costs of education in developing countries by Ta Ngoc Châu (1972)

Qualitative aspects of educational planning (1969)

Research for educational planning: notes on emergent needs by William J. Platt (1970)

Systems approach to teacher training and curriculum development: the case of developing countries by Taher A. Razik (1972)

The following books, produced in but not published by the Institute, are obtainable through normal bookselling channels:

Managing educational costs by Philip H. Coombs and Jacques Hallak
Published by Oxford University Press, New York, London and Toronto, 1972

Quantitative methods of educational planning by Héctor Correa
Published by International Textbook Co., Scranton, Pa., 1969

The world educational crisis: a systems analysis by Philip H. Coombs
Published by Oxford University Press, New York, London and Toronto, 1968

/379.12H669F>C1/